The Commuter's Confessions

poems by

Lucia Melgar

Finishing Line Press
Georgetown, Kentucky

The Commuter's Confessions

For all the commuters, who in time, become the globe's greatest philosophers. May the unseen meditations throughout your collected journeys continue to gift you epiphanies about the mysteries of humankind.

Publisher: Leah Huete de Maines
Editor: Christen Kincaid
Cover Art: Jui Deshpande, "InfiniArtCreations" by Zui
Author Photo: Louis Scott
Cover Design: Elizabeth Maines McCleavy

Order online: www.finishinglinepress.com
also available on amazon.com

Author inquiries and mail orders:
Finishing Line Press
PO Box 1626
Georgetown, Kentucky 40324
USA

Table of Contents

For my great grandmother, Abuelita Maria

Agonized passenger

Not every soul
on the morning train
is tired of the groggy
and ever repetitive ritual of the
Monday morning routine.
Some are inherently miserable—
traveling to a location
And carrying their woes,
like extra socks for their
forever tormented rainy weather.
Being torn and making it felt so,
These travelers murmur soft
curses and whispers of agony,
to an audience of none.
To an audience of working bees,
that buzz only to their own interests.
Be thankful to the doings of nature
if your luggage only carries
your necessities of the mundane,
and not of the necessities of the troubled.

Drained

I am tired
but I am not
allowed to be.
I am drained
but I am not
allowed to be.
I am exhausted.
My limbs want to rest
but they are not
allowed to rest.
My mind wants to halt chugging
it's constant struggle
of unwanted problems,
but it is not
allowed to stop.
I am only
Allowed to continue,
Allowed to continue,
Allowed to continue.

Window

Beyond the small
circular stains of dirt
of the train window
houses have not
been awakened.
Their worries,
immaterial.
Their lives,
dreams.

Heavy Eyes

The bags beneath my eyes
are filled with doubt and ambition.
They are heavy and steep.
I am trying to pull my eyelids
like heavy and dark
velvet curtains,
covering a large window.
Stopping the sunshine—
stopping the clarity,
of the daily journey ahead.

Missed Train

That feeling you get
as you miss your train,
and its poignant doors
close firmly.
First,
you are startled
and frustrated.
Then,
you are understanding
that destiny
tells you not to go.
It tells you there are
more trains to come.

The Commuter's Prayer

Dear Lord,
give me the resiliency
to come back from
the setbacks of the workplace.
Give me the inspiration
to see beyond the
duties of today's job.
Give me the courage,
to fight through these
strenuous hours of labor.
Give me the energy
to not underestimate
my own will and competence.
Through the motion of this train,
and through my sorrows of my dreams
I pray.
Amen.

All Seats Taken

There is no space
for me on this train.
As full as the heart of
a person who
cannot and will not love.
When all hope is diminished,
and everyone seems
like empty hearted fools—
there is always a tired soul
with diming sweetness,
helping out another
disappointed one.

End of the Tracks

The mornings in which
you feel that you can conquer—
you feel that it's fine.
That the job is worth it.
Versus the feeling of deviating from
what you are and what you want
your future self to become,
are the most confusing to me.
Have I accepted my fate?
Have I given up on seeking my divine sign?
Is this it?

The Weekend

Like a memory that
you never want to let go,
I am writing a poem
about Friday
on Monday.
It's warm and fun,
buzzing with a low hum.
Until next time my dear day friend.

One with the train

This feeling of nothingness
and boundless boredom,
is heavy against my chest.
It swings to the rhythm
of this old train.
Lightness is something I strive to find,
a place in my existence were
the heaviness dissipates
like a long-forgotten thought.

Train Steam

Why do I have ephemeral motivations filled with steam?
These in a blue moon emotions,
that bring me to an obsessive state.
An unstable quality that is broken easily,
just as the weakened leaves plunge in the fall.
What must I do—to find
my eternal consuming and ruling fixation?
Let me follow it to the ends of this universe.
Without doubt and without fear.

Music Tracks

Instead of the popular upbeat tracks of my time,
I have been railing into a hollow to easily shield me.
I fear of my youthful spirit disappearing
and becoming another one of those.
Those whose inner child has been removed,
and boarded away from their thoughts and actions.
I have been instead attending to music of my childhood.
I listen and try to find the broken pieces of the rhetoric of my infant
self.
I listen to comfort myself, as I head to a place of silenced children.

Ode to my ticket

Ah, my dear and small piece of tree—
you take me to places that I want and don't want to go.
You are the one who dictates my way.
You are the one that bends my knee.
With you I will continue to grow.
With you, my love, things will stay the same—
even if my innocence is melting away.
May the thoughts, prayers, and visions in these passages—
never become mundane and tamed!
My dear pass to the city—
may your round edges and colorful exterior,
emulate the hopes and dreams that vibrate inside my soul.

Locomotive Lies

Stop fabricating the stories of your life
to please others, rail rider!
Here as the tram pushes past time,
you remember that the stories
you have told
have mundanity,
rather than glory.
Don't be ashamed that living—
is more than dreaming.
Existing is evangelical.
Interacting can be as familiar
as the repetitive road you always take.

Incorrect Terminals

The week.
It seems endless.
When will my rest begin?
Let the healing of these
tired and droopy eyes dawn.
When will I begin to chortle?
When will I start
to connect to the terminal
of my heart,
and not that of my mind?
When will the demand
of my inner self take over
the tedious turnpikes
of the workplace?

Not the Express Weekend

This is the beginning,

of a long weekend.
Three extended days—
as lasting as the rides with
all the local stops.
Recuperating with the wind of the late summer breeze.
Healing through the amiable rays of the sun.
Acquiring vitality through the underpass of the moon.
Maybe after this minuscule retirement,
I can uncover more will
hiding under my skin—
to continue ahead.

The Gap between the Platform and the Train

I feel that I don't have the strength
to do this anymore.
I wish that I could drown—
within the gap between the train and the platform.
My motivation is being
slowly dragged by the dirty rainwater
cleaning my window.
I am again at the alpha
of this interminable ride.
I am again lost and not knowing my end.
How to find the power to operate
something that you don't want to do!
Please help me find the way to
whatever it is I must find the way to.
Please help me inspire
my senses to look beyond the present.

Stations and Society

Recognizing a stranger,
is like recognizing a long-lost friend—
that you have never met before.
To feel comfortable in a sea of strangers.
To feel kin with unknown faces.
To feel care where you least expect it.
It is the recognition of the humanity,
in each and every one of us.
The kinship of commuters.
We are what society endeavors.
We are the utopia you need.

Dead Train

The train lost its power.
The brakes screeched.
The lights were out.
Breathing from slightly angry
and fatigued passengers became
prominent and heavy.
You could hear it, just as you
can see breathing form in the frosty mornings.
The train has stopped, the routine was killed.
When will it pick up?
When will it become alive once more?

Passenger's Personal Space

My hip is twisted to the side
and refuses to straighten
next to this siting stranger.
The stranger is an outlier.
The type that deters from—
the slightest touch of the hip to happen.

He wouldn't have this innocent unavoidable contact.
There is a border drawn within the space
where the air of my perfume and his cologne mix.

Some individuals protect their air land.
They collect world they don't own.
They act as landlords, but with no land.
Be careful in safeguarding what is not yours.
Hoarding what you can't take away.

Cheerful Uniform

The week is concluding
and I am slumped against
my upright positioned berth—
in a berry-colored outfit.
I want to be just as colorful
as these dusty rose rayon trousers.
Just as warm
as this deep burgundy blouse.
My body is a streetcar without desire.
It is lively and lifeless.
It is wanting and un-wanting.
It is ready for the day
to end its course.

Railroad Car Aromas

The smells of the train are many.
They are sometimes fresh and floral.
Sweet and stunning.
Sometimes they even make—
your morning aching stomach grumble.
But most of the time they are—
stingy and strong.
They smell of work and dirt on outdated leather.
They make my head spin.
They make my nose tremor.
They make me want to turn tail.
They remind me of where I am.
But not of where I am going.

No reservations

Must I accept now,
that the world is
filled with uncertainty.
My seat aboard the train is not reserved.
My alarm clock ring is not always guaranteed.
My decisions are never known to be the best.

My life's course is not written in permanent ink,
but in a light mechanical pencil—
which even when erased, leaves
indentations in the glue-white paper.
I believe I have cracked the most
desirable quality of every human's existence.
They want to know.
They want to completely know.

What is right.
What is wrong.
What will happen.
They want to get rid of uncertainty just as one
gets rid of emotional heaviness when confessing a sin.
Can this be?
Are there citizens that have more certainty than others?
Or must we be prepared, to never really-
really know if there are sharks or a field of flowers
as we turn the steep hills of life?
Are we destined to enjoy life through dirty glasses?

Conductors

The sound of the conductor
stamping tickets approaches.
The sound awakens my senses.
This conductor has spared me.
He has violently pulled me from a place
that I have never been before.
A fantasy derailing from logic.
His warning announced my reality.
It alarmed me of my ungratefulness.
I was able to get on the train,
to have economic dignity.
Its sound presages society
that you are on the way to work.
True, my dear commuter but
it also advises that it is a new day.
A day in which anything can
and will happen
A day where you can have
an epiphany that changes it all,
or a grand force of motivation.
Don't underestimate
the sound of the railroad hole punch,
creating gaps between your ticket and your pleas.
It is a privilege to hear it.

Autumn is all aboard

I used to see the window's
charming display of freckles of dirt
through the sunlight of the morning sky.
But Autumn is now at this juncture,
and I give faith that it is the
gloomiest of turns in a commuter's life.
Now, not only is there a journey ahead
every morning and every night,
but it is now buried and encompassed
in an icy, dim, and indigo background.
My heart wails for
that round globe of heat in the sky.
It weeps for its warmth to coddle me.
It weeps in the abyss of frost.

Advertisement Aging

There is no better way—
to look upon the passing of time,
than with the poster boards placed
throughout the train station platform.
They tell you what's new and what's upcoming.
They remind you that what you are today, you weren't yesterday.
They hold the events of the future in your repetitive present.
They tell you that all things pass, even though,
you think you are not crusading forward.
They remind you like a fall-colored tree
you admire from your car window.
That you are here.
That you are here.
That you are here.

Lucia Melgar was born in Norwalk, CT and has lived all over the United States including San Diego, Tampa, and San Antonio. Lucia is a first generation Guatemalan American and always strives to derive inspiration of her culture. Poetry is in her blood, one of the most prized possessions is a picture of her great grandmother performing in a poetry competition. Every generation in her family has been involved in poetry and uses poetry in everyday communication. She went to college in Sacred Heart University in Fairfield, CT and studied Finance. After college, she worked Goldman Sachs, where poetry was not really considered a forte. Some may not agree, but Finance actually enhanced her poetry writing abilities and caused her to yearn a life of words and romanticism. She has been published in the *NYU SPS Dovetail,* Issue Fall 2020. She loves to travel and believes that everyone should read Pablo Neruda before they die.